I0814767

So Lucky You're My Mom

LET ME TELL YOU WHY

MOM—DO you KNOW WHAT
I JUST REALIZED?
My LIFE IS PRETTY GREAT.

AND DO YOU KNOW WHO HAD SOMETHING TO DO WITH THAT?

YOU!

LET ME TELL YOU WHY.

THIS BOOK IS A CELEBRATION OF *you*—
A GREAT *Big* CHEER
FOR ALL YOU'VE DONE FOR ME
AND A PARTY FOR ALL WE'VE SHARED.

I'VE FILLED IT WITH MY FAVORITE THINGS ABOUT YOU,

THE VERY BEST MEMORIES I HAVE OF YOU,

PLUS ALL THE THINGS YOU DO THAT AMAZE ME, IMPRESS ME, AND MAKE ME FEEL CAPABLE OF ANYTHING—BECAUSE...

____

____.

MY WHOLE LIFE,
I'VE HAD A
FRONT ROW SEAT
TO YOUR
MAGIC.

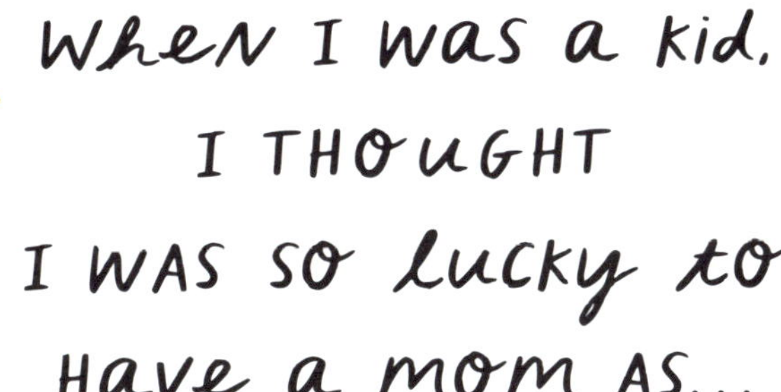

- [ ] CARING
- [ ] HILARIOUS
- [ ] STRONG
- [ ] SMART
- [ ] HIP
- [ ] SUPPORTIVE
- [ ] WISE
- [ ] ADVENTUROUS
- [ ] KNOWLEDGEABLE
- [ ] CREATIVE
- [ ] LOVING
- [ ] THOUGHTFUL
- [ ] PLAYFUL

...as you.

YOU WERE THE ONLY MOM
I KNEW WHO

______________________________,

AND I BRAGGED TO ALL MY
FRIENDS ABOUT YOUR

______________________________.

PLUS, I ALWAYS HAD THE...

(circle one on each side)

BEST	outfits
MOST FUN	meals
COOLEST	stories
WILDEST	advice
SWEETEST	birthday parties
MOST MAGICAL	vacations
MOST LEGENDARY	role model
FUNNIEST	adventures

...THANKS TO you.

GROWING UP,
I LOVED THAT
I GOT TO SEE YOUR

____

SIDE.

LIKE THAT
ONE TIME *you*

____

______________________________________.

How is it that out of ALL the moms in the WORLD, you ended up MINE?

WHEN I WAS YOUNGER,
I THOUGHT you MADE

____

LOOK SO EASY.

AS I GOT OLDER,
I REALIZED HOW INCREDIBLY

____

you REALLY WERE.

REMEMBER MY

____

PHASE?

Yikes.

IS NOW A GOOD TIME TO SAY SORRY FOR

______________________________?

(Really.)

ON THE HARD DAYS, you COULD'VE...

- ☐ PACKED ME UP IN A BOX AND SHIPPED ME HALFWAY AROUND THE WORLD
- ☐ SAID NO TO EVERYTHING FOR THE REST OF TIME
- ☐ GIVEN UP AND SET ME FREE IN THE FOREST
- ☐ TAKEN THE NEXT FLIGHT TO SPAIN AND NEVER COME BACK

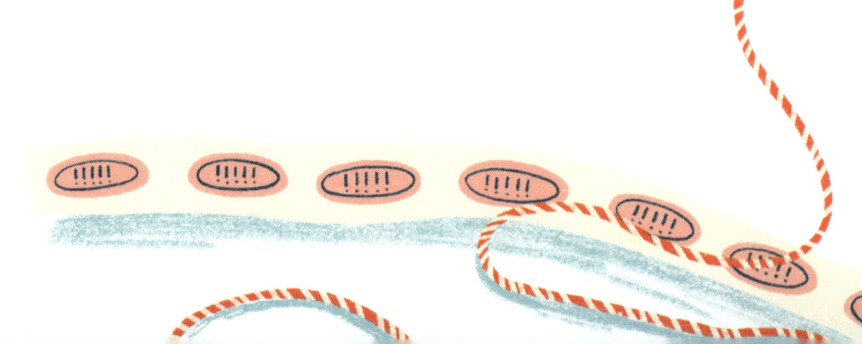

...BUT you DIDN'T.
(THANKS!)

INSTEAD, you

____________________________.

I KNOW, I KNOW,
you're MY MOM—
IT'S your job.

BUT I'VE NEVER FELT MORE LOVED AND SUPPORTED THAN WHEN you

____.

...AND You STILL MAKE ME FEEL 100 FEET TALL, EVERY TIME you

____.

YOU AND ME?
WE'RE LIKE MUSHROOMS—
SNEAKILY CONNECTED
JUST BENEATH THE SURFACE.

I MEAN, I GET SOME OF
MY BEST QUALITIES
FROM YOU:
1.
2.

...AND PROBABLY SOME OF MY WEIRDEST, SUCH AS

_______________________________________.

I LOVE CALLING YOU WHENEVER SOMETHING BIG HAPPENS, LIKE ______________________________.

BUT YOU'RE THERE FOR THE EVERYDAY STUFF TOO, LIKE...

1. ______________________________

2. ______________________________

3. ______________________________

HERE'S THE THING—YOU MAY THINK I'M GROWN UP, BUT I STILL NEED YOUR...

- ☐ REGULAR CHATS
- ☐ LEVEL-HEADED ADVICE
- ☐ WARM HUGS
- ☐ FIVE-STAR COOKING
- ☐ LITTLE PEP TALKS
- ☐ BIG IDEAS
- ☐ ______________________

...TO GET ME THROUGH.

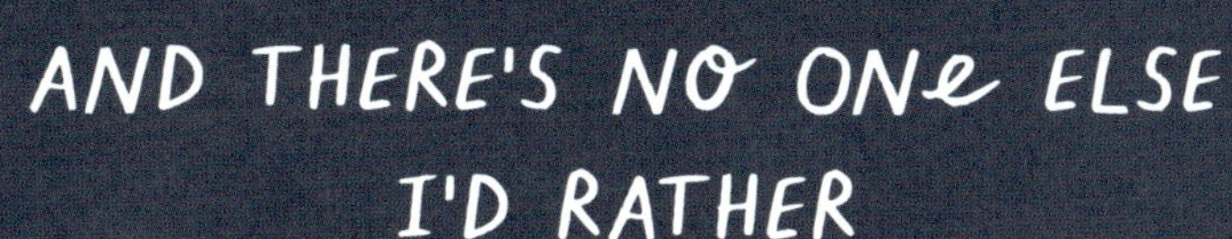

AND THERE'S NO ONE ELSE
I'D RATHER

WITH THAN *you*. (TRULY!)

THE WILD THING IS, YOU'RE NOT <u>JUST</u> MY MOM.

YOU HAVE A WHOLE INSPIRING LIFE DRIZZLED ON TOP.

WHEN I WAS A KID, I WAS FASCINATED BY ALL THE THINGS YOU MADE TIME FOR (JUST FOR YOU), LIKE...

1.

2.

3.

...AND I watched YOU WORK hard TO

______________________________.

REMEMBER WHEN YOU WANTED TO TRY SOMETHING NEW AND ____________________?

I THOUGHT THAT WAS SO COOL.

LOOKING BACK, IT'S CLEAR YOUR PASSION FOR

____

RUBBED OFF ON ME.

IF I HAD TO LIST YOUR BIGGEST ACHIEVEMENTS, THEY WOULD BE:

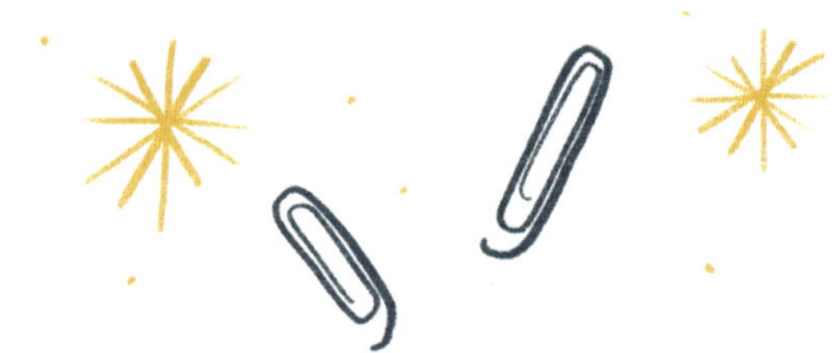

1. ME (OF COURSE)

2. __________

3. __________

4. __________

SEE WHAT I MEAN?

Impressive stuff.

BUT WHAT I LOVE MOST IS THAT you STILL FIND ROOM IN your SCHEDULE (AND HEART) FOR ME.

WITH ALL THE TIME YOU SPEND

________________________________,

AND ALL THE FUN YOU NOW HAVE

________________________________.

...BECAUSE WE'VE GOT PLACES
LEFT TO GO,
PUZZLES TO PIECE TOGETHER,
AND TREASURES STILL TO UNCOVER.

IF I STRUCK IT RICH,
I'D TAKE YOU

______________________________.

We'd BRING

____

AND PASS THE days

______________________________.

But I DON'T NEED A CENT
TO HAVE A GOOD TIME WITH YOU—

just______________________________

AND______________________________.

IF I COULD REWIND THE CLOCK, I'D WANT TO RELIVE THE DAY WE

____

____

____.

AS WE BOTH GET OLDER...

I HOPE WE CAN

____

______________________________.

...AND I HOPE

WE NEVER STOP

____

______________________________.

MOM—YOU MAKE ME FEEL LUCKY. LUCKY TO HAVE ENDED UP EXACTLY WHERE I NEED TO BE:

- ☐ MAKING MOVES AND DOING RAD THINGS
- ☐ CONTRIBUTING TO THE WORLD IN MY OWN WAY
- ☐ DREAMING BIG ABOUT WHAT'S NEXT
- ☐ COZY IN THIS LIFE I'M BUILDING
- ☐ SECURE AND LOVED NO MATTER WHAT

I DON'T SAY IT ENOUGH,
BUT IT'S TRUE:

____

______________________________.

THE TRUTH IS...
WITHOUT YOU,
I WOULDN'T BE ME.

THANKS FOR (PRETTY MUCH)
EVERYTHING.

WITH LOVE, ________________

(A VERY LUCKY PERSON)

Written by: Danielle Leduc McQueen
Illustrated by: Kerrie McNeill
Edited by: Bailey Vega
Art Directed by: Megan Gandt

ISBN: 978-1-957891-36-1

1st printing. Printed in China with soy inks on FSC®-Mix certified paper.

Create meaningful moments with gifts that inspire.

CONNECT WITH US
live-inspired.com | sayhello@compendiuminc.com

@compendiumliveinspired
#compendiumliveinspired